ZIGGY & ME

Publication Details
ZIGGY & ME
978-1-64633-840-5
Copyright: Jill Parris
The moral rights of the authors has been asserted. All rights reserved, Without limiting the rights under copyright restricted above, no part of this publication may be reproduced into a retrieval system, or be transmitted, in any form or by any means (electronic, mechanical, photocopying, recording or otherwise), without the prior written permission of both the copyright owner and the publisher of this book.
Published by Parris Publishing
Cover picture: ZIGGY by ill Parris

This book is dedicated to
Aahil, Toto
&
Ziggy the Cat

When I was little I used to bounce
To bounce and pounce and jump for joy
Dash through tunnels
Or run after mice
Jump at feathers
Or hiss at your smile
I'd roll into the tightest ball
And mew out loud
At the dinner call.

Now I am bigger and almost grown up
I am learning to carry myself like a cat.

This kitten likes playing
On his tummy and back
He creeps and he stalks
And then hides and attacks
He tumbles
   and rumbles
      and hangs
         upside down

And sometimes
  in fun
     for no reason at all
  he bites and he
scratches
like a spiky hiss ball.

So watch out!
Keep eyes peeled! For that glint in his eye
The swipe of the paw or the nip on your shin
A scratch from a claw meant simply in fun
As he draws all attention entirely to Him!

Now little Ziggy has grown quite a bit
His moods are so many - Not sure how they fit
So let's look very carefully and perhaps we will see
If any of these
Look the same as in me.

When Ziggy's feeling happy
He purrs for all he's worth
He rubs you with his head
Until you smile and laugh.

Sometimes Ziggy's very sad
Like when his best friend Floodle leaves
He sits down on the doorstep
It's the only place to grieve.

He sits there for a long, long time
Just staring at the door
Then comes and asks to cuddle
To help forget it all.

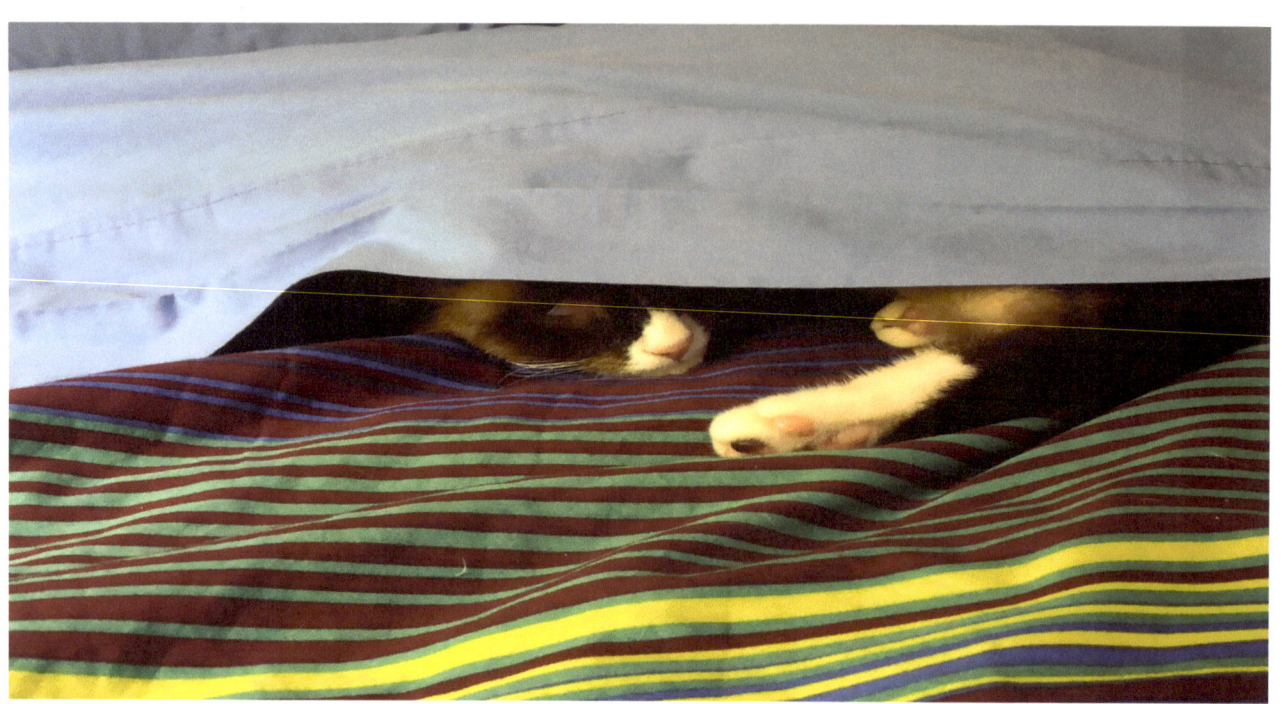

Playing under sheets is fun

It's **such** great fun

You can hide out of sight,
    Wait long as you like
        Wait until you're forgotten.

Then, you can slowly creep out
    And pounce and bounce
        Yes pounce and bounce
            And get that toe
                Yes get that toe

        And hold it tight
      Or pull and bite
    Yes pull that toe
With all your might

Until the man sits bolt upright
And demands that you give up the fight.

Ziggy **loves** being naughty
To him it's just good fun
Biting at a cushion
Or offering his tum
Just so that he can kick and bite
At your fingers or your thumbs

With claws and teeth that prickle
And paws and claws that snatch.
He's inviting you to tickle
So he can bite and scratch.

His eyes light up
He's having fun
And if it hurts
Well then - **Who me?**
A cuddly cat
Just full of fun.

Not one mean bone at all
In this furry one.

So watch right out
For mouth and paws
Cute little Ziggy
All teeth and claws.

Yes our Ziggy
All teeth and claws.

After his walk
And his after walk treat
Ziggy is off to his basket
To have a long sleep.

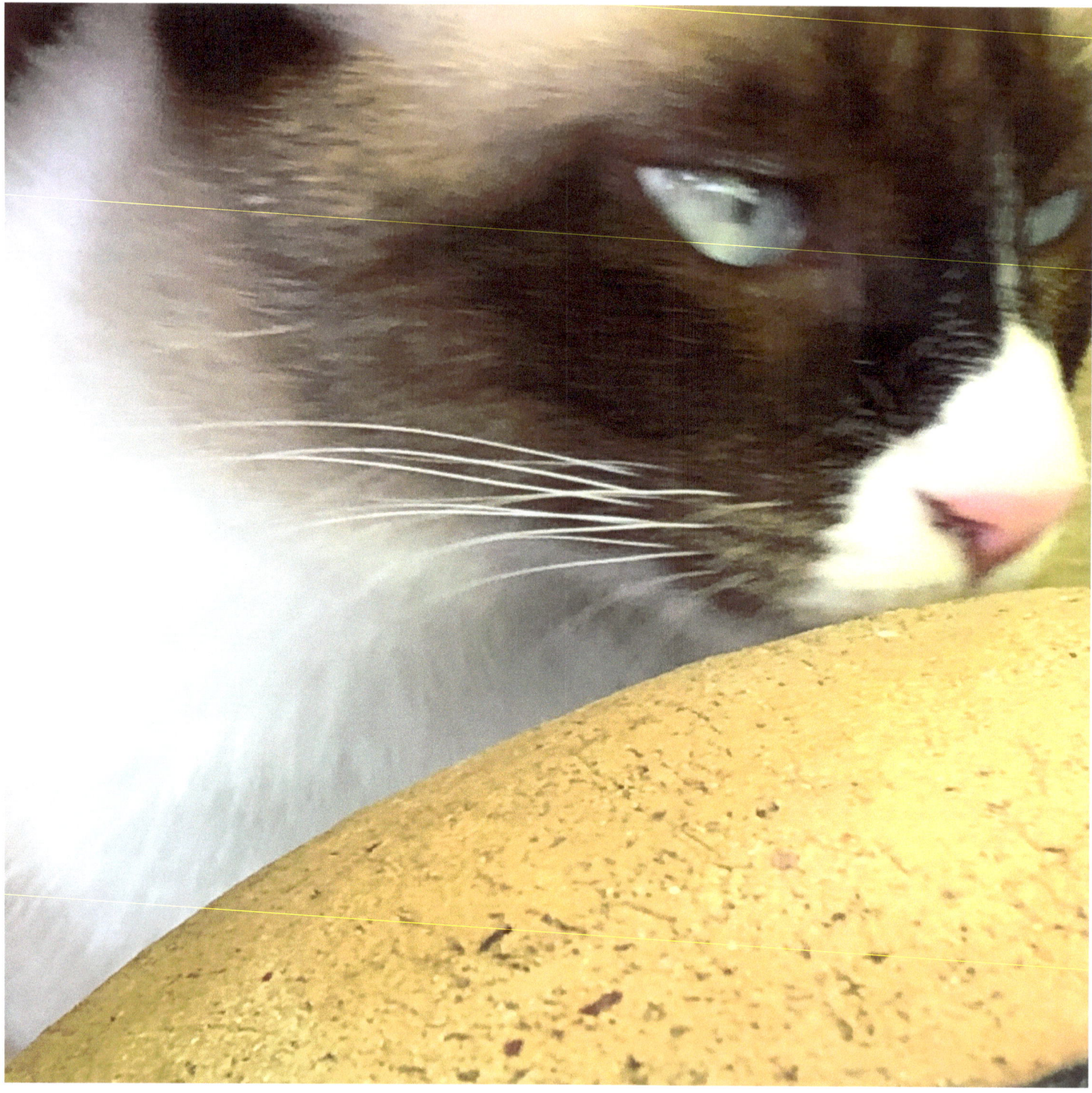

Ziggy can be very shy
And some days he just wants to hide
It's just as if he's scared to turn
And look you in the eye.

So if this happens to you one day
If you feel funny in your tummy
Don't be scared
Cause you're feeling weird
Just remember that Ziggy
          that great big fluff ball
          has times when he won't
          look at anyone at all.

Ziggy is a friendly cat
Who loves to bounce and play
With paper balls, toy mice
And crinkled tinsel paper

And if invited
He will jump
Into a bowl
That tasty lump!

His favorite bowl
The big blue one
You can see him here
He's having fun.

Yes Ziggy is a friendly cat
Who likes to play

And that is that.

Today Ziggy is an angry cat
You can see because his tail is fat
And Floodle looks quite scared of him
See his ears and eyes and his sheepish grin.

Or perhaps for Zig it's all in fun
A playful rage out in the sun.

Ziggy is hungry and when he is
He yells until you stop and listen.
He doesn't care about dinner time
Says feed me **now** and I'll be fine.

When he's finished he will wash his face
Then purrs and snuggles around the place.

I think Ziggy is frightened
Because his eyes are big and round
And Floodle looks quite anxious
I wonder **What's that sound?**

When you get a fright what do you do?
Do your eyes get big, do you listen too?
Do you run and hide right out of sight?
Or say out loud

"No! I won't do that!"

Ziggy is looking friendly
As friendly as can be
And the Kooke seems quite curious
Thinking has he come to play with me.

Well if I was Kooka I wouldn't get too chummy
And Ziggy watch out for **his** beak
It's big and sharp
And he likes meat.
First have a chat - that distance is fine
You can meet again some other time.

Ziggy loves Floodle and Floodle loves Zig
That's why they rub foreheads
And run and call and play
And then when the are tired
Of running up and down
They cuddle up together
And sleep without a sound.

Well now that I've told you
About Ziggy the cat
I wonder what feelings
You have under your hat?

Do you dream of being Hungry
Or Sleepy or Shy?
Do you cry, laugh out loudly
Without knowing why?

And before going to bed
Do you ask for this book
And enjoy all the things
Ziggy does?
Do you **look?**

Sleep well little person
If you're off to bed
And remember my Ziggy
Loves to be in your head.

THE END

www.ingramcontent.com/pod-product-compliance
Lightning Source LLC
Chambersburg PA
CBHW041124070526
44584CB00003B/275